# OXFORD SPELLING

Dr Tessa Daffern

**STUDENT BOOK 6**

Name: _____

Class: _____

**OXFORD**
UNIVERSITY PRESS
AUSTRALIA & NEW ZEALAND

**OXFORD**
UNIVERSITY PRESS

Oxford University Press is a department of the University of Oxford.
It furthers the University's objective of excellence in research,
scholarship, and education by publishing worldwide. Oxford is a registered
trademark of Oxford University Press in the UK and in certain other
countries.

Published in Australia by
Oxford University Press
Level 8, 737 Bourke Street, Docklands, Victoria 3008, Australia.

© Oxford University Press 2021

The moral rights of the author have been asserted

First published 2021
Reprinted 2022, 2023 (four times), 2024

ISBN 9780190326142

**Reproduction and communication for educational purposes**
The Australian *Copyright Act 1968* (the Act) allows educational institutions that
are covered by remuneration arrangements with Copyright Agency to reproduce
and communicate certain material for educational purposes. For more information,
see copyright.com.au.

Edited by Lucy Ridsdale
Cover illustration by Lisa Hunt
Illustrated by Becky Davies
Typeset by Integra Software Services Pvt. Ltd., Pondicherry, India
Proofread by Anita Mullick
Printed in China by Golden Cup Printing Co Ltd

Oxford University Press Australia & New Zealand is committed to
sourcing paper responsibly.

MIX
Paper | Supporting
responsible forestry
FSC
www.fsc.org
FSC™ C110497

**Acknowledgements**
The author and the publisher wish to thank the following copyright holders for reproduction of their material.

*A Day to Remember* by Jackie French, HarperCollins Children's Books, 2014, pp. 14, 18, 22; *One Small Island: The
Story of Macquarie Island* by Alison Lester, Penguin Books, Australia, 2019, pp. 30, 34; *The Glimme* by Emily Rodda,
Omnibus Books from Scholastic Australia, 2019, pp. 74, 89; Shutterstock, pp. 29, 30, 34

The 'Bringing it together' activities provided online are adapted with permission from Daffern, T. (2018).
*The components of spelling: Instruction and assessment for the linguistic inquirer.* Literacy Education Solutions Pty Limited.

Every effort has been made to trace the original source of copyright material contained in this book. The
publisher will be pleased to hear from copyright holders to rectify any errors or omissions.

# WELCOME TO OXFORD SPELLING

Welcome to *Oxford Spelling Student Book 6*! This book contains 28 units that you will use across the year, and that will help you gain new spelling knowledge and skills.

You will notice that each unit is divided into three sections:

**Phonology (green section)**

**Orthography (blue section)**

**Morphology (purple section).**

This has been done to guide you in the types of thinking you might use to answer the questions in each section.

> **Tip**
> - **In the phonology sections, think about the sounds you can hear in words.**
> - **In the orthography sections, think about the letter patterns that you know.**
> - **In the morphology sections, think about the meaning of base words, prefixes and suffixes.**

At the end of each unit, your teacher will work with you on a 'Bringing it together' activity. This is a chance to bring together all the things you are learning about spelling and apply them to new words!

Your teacher, along with the *Oxford Spelling* superheroes, will be giving you lots of helpful information as you work through this book. Look out for the tips in each unit for handy hints on how to answer questions.

Enjoy *Oxford Spelling,* and meet the two superheroes who will help you become super spellers – Cloudy Charley and Lightning Lily!

# UNIT 1

**Tip**

Each syllable must contain a vowel phoneme.
For instance, the word 'context' has two syllables: the first, 'con', has a **short /o/** vowel and the second, 'text', has a **short /e/** vowel.

**1** Say each word and count the syllables. Write each word in the correct row of the table and count the number of phonemes it has.

chlorine    cautious    thoughtfully    augmentation    automatically

autonomous    pause    precaution    force    notoriously

| | Word | How many phonemes? |
|---|---|---|
| One-syllable words | | |
| Two-syllable words | | |
| Three-syllable words | | |
| Four-syllable words | | |
| Five-syllable words | | |

**Tip**

Remember to check the meaning of any unfamiliar spelling terms in the glossary. Glossary terms are highlighted in orange.

OXFORD UNIVERSITY PRESS

1 There are many ways to spell the **/aw/** phoneme (as in 'fork'). The table below shows some of the most common letter patterns involving this phoneme. Use these letter patterns to help you fill in the missing letters in the words. Write each completed word in the table and underline the letter pattern involving the **/aw/** phoneme.

s_____ness          n_____mal          br_____t          g_____met          _____ful

inst_____          carniv_____          _____dience          rew_____d          outd_____

d_____way          w_____k          t_____nament          th_____tful          ass_____tment

expl_____          p_____se          tow_____ds          cardb_____d          h_____k

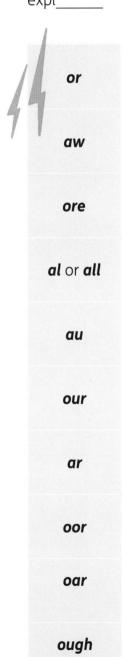

| or |
| --- |
| aw |
| ore |
| al or all |
| au |
| our |
| ar |
| oor |
| oar |
| ough |

**1** Use the homophones to complete the sentences. You may use a dictionary to help you.

horse/hoarse    course/coarse

source/sauce    sore/saw/soar

a   I squirted barbecue _____ onto my sausage sandwich.

b   A _____ is a tool that can be used to cut wood.

c   Scientists predict temperatures will _____ to record levels this summer.

d   Biomass is a renewable energy _____.

e   The _____ grazed in the paddock.

f   The sailor had trouble keeping the yacht on _____ during the storm.

g   My voice sounds _____ from the constant coughing.

h   The texture of sandpaper can be described as _____.

i   I _____ mountains on the horizon.

j   The physiotherapist suggested stretching so I don't feel so _____ after running.

OXFORD UNIVERSITY PRESS

**2**  Write your own sentences using the homophones.

| | |
|---|---|
| hoarse | |
| horse | |
| course | |
| coarse | |
| source | |
| sauce | |
| sore | |
| saw | |
| soar | |

Now try this unit's 'Bringing it together' activity, which your teacher will give you.

# UNIT 2

A disyllabic word is a word made up of two syllables. 'Pumpkin' and 'winter' are disyllabic words.

**1** Say each word and clap out the syllables. Notice that each word is disyllabic. In some of the words, the first syllable is accented (the beat feels stronger). In the others, the accented syllable is the second one. Sort the words using the table.

| intent | cartoon | magnet | perceive | garden | involve | number |

| napkin | tonight | invent | winter | pumpkin | return | native |

| window | combine | entice | monkey | include | pencil |

| First syllable is accented | Second syllable is accented |
| --- | --- |
|  |  |

A grapheme is another word for a letter pattern. It is a letter or group of letters that represents one speech sound.
The word 'shell' has three graphemes: **sh**, **e** and **ll**.

1 There are a few ways to spell the **/n/** phoneme (as in 'no'). Find the grapheme that represents the **/n/** phoneme in each word and sort the words using the chart.

gnaw   knobbly   technical   annual   punnet   assigned   transform

convey   knew   spanner   sovereign   gnarl   enticed   knowledge

channel   knitted   design   funnel   knives   knotted   balance

resign   innovate   window

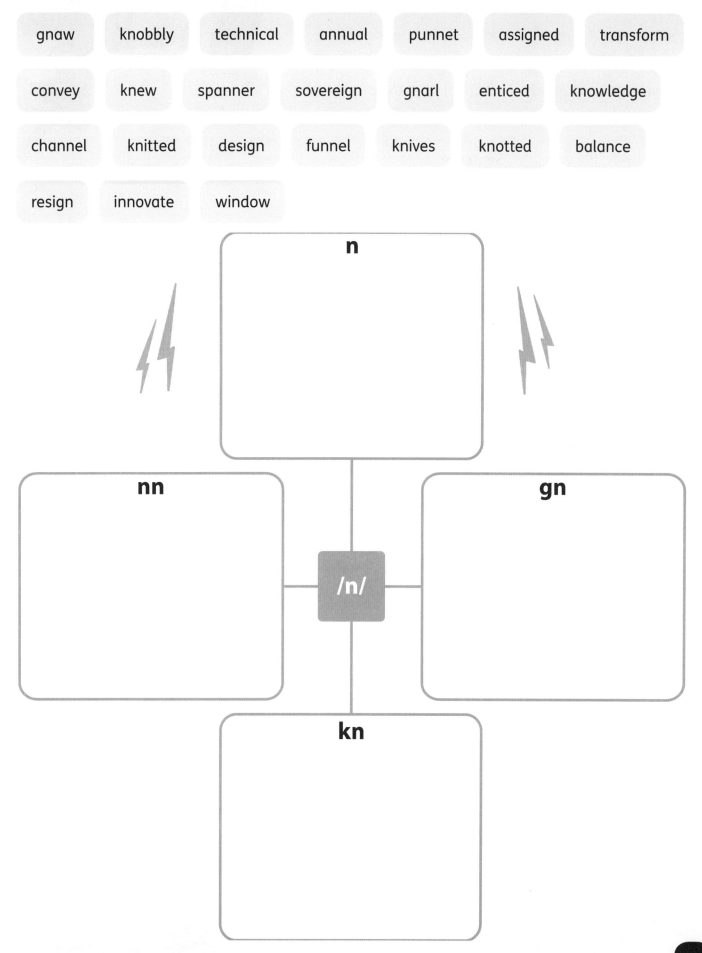

**n**

**nn**

**gn**

**/n/**

**kn**

**2** Write these words in alphabetical order and write a sentence for each of them. You may use a dictionary to help you.

| spanner | gnaw | knobbly | assignment |

| sovereign | gnarl | annual | transform |

Word                    Sentence

**1** Use the homophones to complete the sentences. You may use a dictionary to help you.

weather/whether    cue/queue

knot/not    knead/need

a    The potter will _____ the clay before constructing a sculpture.

**b** My teacher gave us a _____ to start packing our bags.

**c** I tied my shoelaces with a double _____ .

**d** A synoptic chart provides information about

the _____ .

**e** We _____ to wear our hats when we go outside for recess.

**f** My touch football team is _____ training during the holidays.

**g** We couldn't decide _____ to go for a walk or to go on a bike ride.

**h** There was a long _____ of people waiting to be served at the post office.

**2** Write your own sentences using the homophones.

| weather | |
|---|---|
| whether | |
| cue | |
| queue | |
| knot | |
| not | |
| need | |
| knead | |

**Now try this unit's 'Bringing it together' activity, which your teacher will give you.**

OS

**Tip**

A schwa is a type of vowel sound that is neither long nor short. It is an **/uh/** sound.
A schwa is only ever heard in an unaccented syllable. The **a** in 'balloon' represents a schwa sound.

1   Say each word. Can you hear a schwa? Sort the words using the table.

| lady | sleeping | travel | banana | athlete | again | maintain |

| inside | second | robot | perhaps | problem | music | question |

| politics | streamline | fourteen | economic | monsoon | position |

| Words with a schwa | Words without a schwa |
| --- | --- |
|  |  |

2   Underline the consonant blends in the words you wrote in the table.

**Tip**

Remember that a blend can occur at the beginning of a word (as in 'play'), the middle (as in 'acting') or the end (as in 'nest').
A blend can also occur at a syllable juncture, for example, the blend **/ns/** in 'ransom'.

OXFORD UNIVERSITY PRESS

**3** Say each word and count the syllables. Write each word in the correct row of the table and count the number of phonemes it has.

questioning    problematic    musicality    side    second

strain    economical    position    maintain    politician

| | Word | How many phonemes? |
|---|---|---|
| One-syllable words | | |
| Two-syllable words | | |
| Three-syllable words | | |
| Four-syllable words | | |
| Five-syllable words | | |

**Tip**

A diphthong is a kind of long vowel sound that you make by moving your mouth in two ways, such as the **/ow/** sound in the word 'cow'.

The **long /a/**, as in 'spray', the **long /o/**, as in 'boat', and the **long /i/**, as in 'night', are also diphthongs. Notice how your mouth changes shape when you say the **long /a/** phoneme in 'strain' and the **long /i/** phoneme in 'side'.

**1** There are many ways to spell the **long /a/** phoneme (as in 'play'). Find the grapheme that represents the **long /a/** phoneme in each word. Write each grapheme and its matching word in the first two columns of the table, and then write another word with the same grapheme. The first one is done for you.

| ~~disarray~~ | communicate | freight | available | vertebrae |
| obeying | chamber | greatest | matinée | beige |

| Grapheme | Words with this grapheme | |
| --- | --- | --- |
| **ay** | disarr<u>ay</u> | portr<u>ay</u> |

**2** Look again at the words you wrote in the table. Circle the vowel digraphs that represent the **long /a/** phoneme. Underline the quadgraph (a grapheme with four letters) that represents the **long /a/**.

Tip

A graph is a single letter that represents a single phoneme.
In the word 'pie', **p** is a graph.

**1** Use the rules and example words to complete the sentences on the next page that are in the present tense. Remember to add the suffix **-s** or **-es**.

OXFORD UNIVERSITY PRESS

**If the** base word **ends with a** consonant graph, blend **or** digraph, **but not** s, x, z, ch **or** sh, add the suffix -s.    emit | emits    demand | demands

| check | Mum _____ that the door is locked. |
|---|---|

**If the** base word **ends with** s, x, z, ch **or** sh, **or a** consonant trigraph **such as** tch, add the suffix -es.    surpass | surpasses    clash | clashes

| switch | The owner of the house _____ the lights off. |
|---|---|

**If the** base word **ends in a** consonant **and then** y, **change the** y **to** i **and add the** suffix -es.    supply | supplies    copy | copies

| pry | The painter _____ the lid off the paint tin. |
|---|---|

**If the** base word **ends in** e, **just add the** suffix -s.
decline | declines    inflate | inflates

| apologise | If my brother is late, he genuinely _____. |
|---|---|

**2**  Scan a book you are reading to find some base words that follow the rules you learned in the last activity. The words will be verbs. Write each base verb in the table and add the suffix **-s** or **-es**.

| Rule | Example | Similar base verb | Base verb with -s or -es |
|---|---|---|---|
| 1 | emit \| emits |  |  |
| 2 | surpass \| surpasses |  |  |
| 3 | supply \| supplies |  |  |
| 4 | decline \| declines |  |  |

Now try this unit's 'Bringing it together' activity, which your teacher will give you.

## A Day to Remember
### by Jackie French

Amidst courage and confusion inexperienced 'colonials' gained and tried to hold their ground. They failed, but that day a legend had been born. Below them, in what is now known as Anzac Cove, the piles of bodies grew.

**1** Read the text above and find words in it to complete the table.

| | |
|---|---|
| Two words that start with a consonant digraph | |
| Two words with a **long /a/** phoneme | |
| Two words with a **long /i/** phoneme | |
| Two words with five phonemes | |
| Two words that end with an accented syllable | |
| Three words that start with an accented syllable | |
| A word … | |
| with six phonemes | |
| that rhymes with 'stained' | |
| that ends with a consonant blend | |

| | |
|---|---|
| with a **long /e/** phoneme | |
| with a schwa in the final syllable | |
| with five syllables | |

1. There are many ways to spell the **long /e/** phoneme (as in 'see'). Find the grapheme that represents the **long /e/** phoneme in each word. Write each grapheme and its matching word in the first two columns of the table, and then write another word with the same grapheme. You may use a dictionary to check your spelling. The first one is done for you.

| ~~between~~ | feature | egocentric | deplete | diesel | deceit |
|---|---|---|---|---|---|

| Grapheme | Words with this grapheme | |
|---|---|---|
| **ee** | betw<u>ee</u>n | degr<u>ee</u> |

2. Write a descriptive sentence for each word here and on the next page. You may use a dictionary to help you.

| Word | Sentence |
|---|---|
| agreeable | |
| diesel | |
| egocentric | |

| Word | Sentence |
|------|----------|
| deplete | |
| deceit | |
| feature | |

**1** Use the rules about the suffix **-ing** and the example words to complete the sentences.

> **If the** base word **ends with a short** vowel graph **then a** consonant graph, **double the** last letter **and add the** suffix **-ing**.
> commit | committing    forget | forgetting

plan    My parents are _____ a party for their anniversary.

> **If the** base word **ends with x, or with a** consonant blend, digraph **or** trigraph, **just add the** suffix **-ing**.
> match | matching    blast | blasting

flourish    The orange tree is _____ in the sunlight.

> **If the** base word **has a** vowel digraph **in the last** syllable, **just add the** suffix **-ing**.
> bow | bowing    complain | complaining

speak    A scientist will be _____ at the conference.

> **If the** base word **ends in y, or a** vowel digraph, trigraph **or** quadgraph **such as** ow, er, igh **or** eigh **just add the** suffix **-ing**.
> neigh | neighing    flee | fleeing

| simmer | The sauce was _____ on the stove. |

If the base word ends in **e**, and the **e** is not part of a vowel digraph or trigraph, drop the **e** and then add the suffix **-ing**.

**brake | braking**    **relate | relating**

| choose | Lots of my friends are _____ to join the cricket team. |

**2** Scan a book you are reading to find some base words that follow the rules you learned in the last activity. The words will be verbs. Write each base verb in the table and add the suffix **-ing**.

| Rule | Example | Similar base verb | Base verb with the suffix **-ing** |
|---|---|---|---|
| 1 | forget \| forgetting | | |
| 2 | blast \| blasting | | |
| 3 | complain \| complaining | | |
| 4 | flee \| fleeing | | |
| 5 | relate \| relating | | |

**3** Use the homophones 'genes' and 'jeans' to complete the sentences. You may use a dictionary to help you.

**a** In science, we are learning about how _____ affect our development.

**b** I like to wear my comfortable old _____ .

**Now try this unit's 'Bringing it together' activity, which your teacher will give you.**

## A Day to Remember
### by Jackie French

The war had ended. The survivors came home. Weary, battered in mind and body, few spoke of what they had seen.

There was no need for enlistment marches now. But every family in Australia and New Zealand had lost a loved one or seen the faces of those who had come home. And they remembered.

**1** Read the text above and find words in it to complete the table.

| | |
|---|---|
| Four disyllabic words | |
| Three three-syllable words | |
| Four words with a consonant digraph | |
| Four words with four phonemes | |
| Four words that start with an accented syllable | |
| Three words with five phonemes | |
| Two one-syllable words that end with a consonant blend | |
| Two words with a schwa in the second syllable | |

OXFORD UNIVERSITY PRESS

| | |
|---|---|
| Two words with a **long /a/** phoneme | |
| Two words with a **short /a/** phoneme | |
| Two words with a **long /i/** phoneme | |
| Two words with a **short /i/** phoneme | |
| A word ... | |
| that rhymes with 'foam' | |
| that rhymes with 'joke' | |
| that rhymes with 'crows' | |
| with six phonemes | |
| with a **long /e/** phoneme | |
| with a **short /e/** phoneme | |

1 There are many ways to spell the **long /o/** phoneme (as in 'no'). Find the grapheme that represents the **long /o/** phoneme in each word on the next page. Write each grapheme and its matching word in the first two columns of the table, and then write another word with the same grapheme. The first one is done for you.

| borrow | boastful | evoke | avocado | foe | although | bureau |

| Grapheme for the **long /o/** phoneme | Words with this grapheme |
|---|---|
| **ow** | borr<u>ow</u>                                  foll<u>ow</u> |

2 Write a descriptive sentence for each of these words. You may use a dictionary to help you.

| Word | Sentence |
|---|---|
| boastful | |
| woe | |
| avocado | |
| invoke | |
| bureau | |

OXFORD UNIVERSITY PRESS

1. Write sentences for each base word. Add suffixes to the base words in the first column. The first one is done for you.

**Tip**

When adding suffixes to the base words, remember to use the rules that you have learned so far. Have a look at pages 13, 16 and 17 to refresh your memory.

| Base word | Suffix | Sentence |
|---|---|---|
| reveal | -s or -es | The investigation <u>reveals</u> how circuits work. |
| | -ing | He smiled, <u>revealing</u> his braces. |
| destroy | -s or -es | |
| | -ing | |
| resolve | -s or -es | |
| | -ing | |
| slam | -s or -es | |
| | -ing | |
| balance | -s or -es | |
| | -ing | |
| hatch | -s or -es | |
| | -ing | |
| infect | -s or -es | |
| | -ing | |
| stain | -s or -es | |
| | -ing | |

**Now try this unit's 'Bringing it together' activity, which your teacher will give you.**

## A Day to Remember
### by Jackie French

Now, in World War Two, as Australian troops fought German and Italian armies in Europe and the Middle East to save Britain, and as Japanese armies headed towards Australia, Anzac Day was celebrated at the new War Memorial in Canberra for the first time. But with the risk of Japanese bombers flying overhead, there could be no big gatherings anywhere this year.

**1** Read the text above and find words in it to complete the table.

| | |
|---|---|
| Two four-syllable words | |
| Two words that start with a vowel digraph | |
| Two words that start with a consonant blend | |
| Two words with a **long /a/** phoneme | |
| Two words with a **long /e/** phoneme | |
| A word ... | |
| that starts with a **short /a/** phoneme | |
| that rhymes with 'rewards' | |
| with the **long /o/** phoneme | |
| with nine phonemes | |

OXFORD UNIVERSITY PRESS

1. There are many ways to spell the **long /oo/** phoneme (as in 'moon'). Find the grapheme that represents the **long /oo/** phoneme in each word. Write each grapheme and its matching word in first two columns of the table, and then write another word with the same grapheme. The first one is done for you.

| through | gruesome | dilute | jewellery |

| ruby | suitable | who | booster | routine |

| Grapheme | Words with this grapheme | |
| --- | --- | --- |
| **ough** | thr<u>ough</u> | thr<u>ough</u>out |

2. Write a descriptive sentence for each word below and on the next page.

| Word | Sentence |
| --- | --- |
| dilute | |
| gruesome | |

| Word | Sentence |
|------|----------|
| spruik | |
| boulevard | |

**1** Use the rules about the suffix **-ed** and write a sentence in the past tense using one of the example words for each rule.

If the base word ends with a short vowel graph then a consonant graph (other than x), double the last letter and add the suffix -ed.

drip | dripped    plan | planned    rot | rotted

_____

If the base word ends with x, or with a consonant blend, digraph or trigraph, just add the suffix -ed.

march | marched    tilt | tilted    dispatch | dispatched

_____

If the base word has a medial vowel digraph, just add the suffix -ed.

beam | beamed    rain | rained    toil | toiled

_____

If the base word ends in a vowel digraph or trigraph such as ay, ow, er or igh, usually just add the suffix -ed.

remember | remembered    pray | prayed    stow | stowed

_____

OXFORD UNIVERSITY PRESS

**If the base word ends in e, drop the e and then add the suffix -ed.**

refuse | refused    entwine | entwined    glare | glared

**If the base word ends in a consonant then y, change the y to i, and add the suffix -ed.**

simplify | simplified    rely | relied    carry | carried

**2** Scan a book you are reading to find base verbs that follow the rules you learned in the last activity. Write each base verb in the table and add the suffix **-ed**.

| Rule | Example | Similar base verb | Base verb + suffix **-ed** |
|------|---------|-------------------|----------------------------|
| 1 | drip | dripped | | |
| 2 | march | marched | | |
| 3 | beam | beamed | | |
| 4 | remember | remembered | | |
| 5 | refuse | refused | | |
| 6 | simplify | simplified | | |

**3** Use the homophones to complete the sentences.

leased/least    allowed/aloud    rowed/rode/road    bored/board

a    Robin _____ a building so he could open his new café.

b    After school, we are _____ to use the music room.

c    I was excited to try out my new _____ because I had just learned to surf.

d    Niamh _____ the boat across the river using the oars.

**Now try this unit's 'Bringing it together' activity, which your teacher will give you.**

**Tip**

A multisyllabic word has two or more syllables.
'Friendship' and 'creativity' are both multisyllabic words.

**1** Think of some words you know from a subject you're learning about, such as science, history, or health and physical education. Find some interesting or complex words from this topic to complete the table below.

| | |
|---|---|
| Three disyllabic words | |
| Three three-syllable words | |
| Two four-syllable words | |
| Two five-syllable words | |
| Three words with five phonemes | |
| Three words with six phonemes | |
| Three words with seven phonemes | |
| Three words with eight phonemes | |

OXFORD UNIVERSITY PRESS

| | |
|---|---|
| Three words with nine phonemes | |
| A multisyllabic word with a **long /a/** phoneme | |
| A disyllabic word with a **short /a/** phoneme | |
| A multisyllabic word with a **long /e/** phoneme | |
| A disyllabic word with a **short /e/** phoneme | |
| A word ... | |
| that starts with a schwa | |
| with a schwa in the final syllable | |
| with a **long /oo/** phoneme | |
| with an **/aw/** phoneme | |
| that starts with a consonant digraph | |
| that ends with a consonant digraph | |
| that starts with a consonant blend | |
| that ends with a consonant blend | |

1  There are many ways to spell the **long /i/** phoneme (as in 'sight'). Find the grapheme that represents the **long /i/** phoneme in each word. Write each grapheme and its matching word in first two columns of the table, and then write another word with the same grapheme. The first one is done for you.

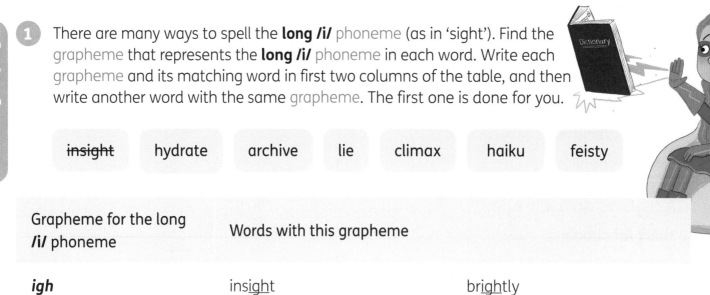

insight   hydrate   archive   lie   climax   haiku   feisty

| Grapheme for the long /i/ phoneme | Words with this grapheme | |
|---|---|---|
| igh | insight | brightly |

2  Write a descriptive sentence for each word. You may use a dictionary to help you.

| Word | Sentence |
|---|---|
| insight | |
| synapse | |
| archive | |
| climax | |

OXFORD UNIVERSITY PRESS

**Tip**

A contraction is a shortened form of two words joined together. An apostrophe is used to replace one or more letters.

The words 'I will' are joined and shortened to make the word 'I'll'. The letters **w** and **i** are replaced with an apostrophe.

**1** Use the homophones to complete the sentences. You may use a dictionary to help you.

| I'll/aisle/isle | he'd/heed | who's/whose | we'll/wheel |

**a** My uncle was trying to remember if _____ left the keys in the car.

**b** A unicycle has one _____ .

**c** I think _____ walk my dog after lunch.

**d** Another word for island is _____ .

**e** My friends and I will have lunch and then

_____ go to the movies together.

**f** My parents want to know _____ shoes are covered in mud.

**g** The farmers were urged to _____ the weather warning.

**h** Our teacher told us _____ coming to visit our class tomorrow.

**i** At the supermarket, I walked down each _____ .

Now try this unit's 'Bringing it together' activity, which your teacher will give you.

## One Small Island: The Story of Macquarie Island
### by Alison Lester

Macquarie Island lies in the Southern Ocean, between Antarctica and New Zealand. A speck of green in the vast, windswept sea, it is a haven for many creatures that live above and below the waves.

The island was born millions of years ago when colossal subterranean forces pushed the sea floor upwards.

Over eons, a ridge rose from the depths until finally its peak broke through the waves. Slowly a whole section of the ocean floor was exposed to form Macquarie Island.

**1** Read the text above and find words in it to complete the table.

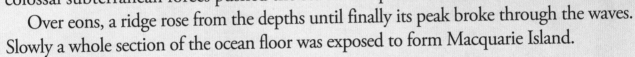

| | |
|---|---|
| Three disyllabic words | |
| Two three-syllable words | |
| A four-syllable word | |
| A five-syllable word | |
| Two words with the same number of phonemes as the word 'colossal' | |
| A word that starts with a consonant blend and ends with a consonant digraph | |
| Three words with a consonant digraph to represent the third phoneme | |

OXFORD UNIVERSITY PRESS

| | |
|---|---|
| All of the words with a **/sh/** phoneme | |
| Two words with a **long /a/** phoneme | |
| A word with a schwa as the second phoneme | |
| Two disyllabic words that start with a consonant blend | |
| All two-syllable words with a **long /e/** phoneme | |
| A three-syllable word with a **long /i/** phoneme | |
| A word with a **long /oo/** phoneme as the third phoneme | |

**1** Write a descriptive sentence for each word. You may use a dictionary to help you.

| Word | Sentence |
|---|---|
| extinguish | |
| machinery | |
| precious | |
| crustacean | |

Orthography

**2** There are many ways to spell the **/sh/** phoneme (as in 'shop'). Find the grapheme that represents the **/sh/** phoneme in each word. Write each grapheme and its matching word in the first two columns of the table, and then write another word with the same grapheme. The first one is done for you.

| ~~extinguish~~ | machinery | section |
| precious | crustacean | mansion |

| Grapheme for the /sh/ phoneme | Words with this grapheme | |
| --- | --- | --- |
| **sh** | extingui<u>sh</u> | <u>sh</u>adow |

**Tip**

The suffix **-ian** can be used to form nouns describing a person. For instance, the word 'music' becomes 'musician', meaning a person who plays music.

**1** Check the spelling of the words shown in the first column of the table below and on the next page. Decide whether they should have the suffix **-ion** or **-ian** and use the correctly spelled word to complete the sentence. Use the tip to help you.

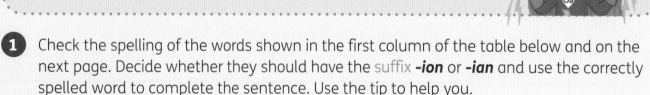

| mathematician | |
| --- | --- |
| mathematicion | A _____ calculates complex equations. |

| | |
|---|---|
| propositian | |
| **proposition** | Our _____ to renovate the building was well received. |
| competition | |
| competitian | Our team won the _____. |
| historion | |
| historian | A _____ studies events that have taken place in the past. |
| musicion | |
| musician | A _____ visited our school and played her oboe. |
| composition | |
| compositian | The sculpture is a unique _____ of clay and wood. |
| pollutian | |
| pollution | Air _____ is reduced because there are fewer vehicles on the road. |
| electrician | |
| electricion | An _____ was required to replace the broken oven. |
| explosian | |
| explosion | A massive _____ shook the ground beneath us. |
| comedion | |
| comedian | The audience laughed hysterically as the _____ performed. |

**Now try this unit's 'Bringing it together' activity, which your teacher will give you.**

# One Small Island: The Story of Macquarie Island
## by Alison Lester

For centuries, animals and plants existed in a fragile balance as the seasons came and went. Megaherbs and tussocks covered the misty hills and jagged rocks towered over stony beaches. There were no trees, and on the wind-scoured plateau, moss and lichen grew in stripes.

**1** Read the text above and find words in it to complete the table.

| | |
|---|---|
| Three words with the same number of phonemes as the word 'plateau' | |
| A word that starts and ends with a consonant blend | |
| Three disyllabic words with a consonant digraph to represent the third phoneme | |
| All of the words that start with a **/s/** phoneme and end with a **/z/** phoneme | |
| A word with a schwa as the third phoneme | |
| A word that rhymes with 'ragged' | |
| All disyllabic words with a **long /e/** phoneme | |
| Three disyllabic words with the **long /o/** phoneme | |

**1** There are many ways to spell the **/s/** phoneme (as in 'sat'). Find the letter patterns that involve this sound in each word. Write each letter pattern and its matching word in the first two columns of the table, and then write another word with the same letter pattern. The first one is done for you.

mystical    colossal    purpose    resource

scenic    gristle    psychology    incident

| Letter pattern | Words with this letter pattern involving the **/s/** phoneme | |
| --- | --- | --- |
| **s** | my_s_tical | _s_addle |

**2** Write a descriptive sentence for each of the words below and on the next page. You may use a dictionary to help you.

| Word | Sentence |
| --- | --- |
| mystical | |
| resource | |

| Word | Sentence |
|------|----------|
| incident | |
| scenic | |

**Tip**

The suffixes **-ance** and **-ence** derive from Latin. They usually refer to a quality or state, but sometimes can mean an action or a process. The word 'performance', with the suffix **-ance**, means 'the process of performing'. The word 'persistence', with the suffix **-ence**, means 'the state of persisting'.

**Morphology**

**1** Use the rules below and on the next page to complete the table on the next page.

**If the base word is a verb that ends in *y*, change the *y* to *i* and add the suffix -*ance*.**

apply | appliance    rely | reliance    defy | defiance

**If the base word is a verb that ends in *ure*, remove the final *e* and add the suffix -*ance*.**

insure | insurance    reassure | reassurance    nurture | nurturance

**If the base word is a verb that ends in *ear*, add the suffix -*ance*.**

forbear | forbearance    reappear | reappearance

**If the base word is an adjective that ends in *ant*, remove these three graphemes and add the suffix -*ance*.**

tolerant | tolerance    elegant | elegance    fragrant | fragrance

OXFORD UNIVERSITY PRESS

If the base word is an adjective that ends in *ent*, remove these three letters and add the suffix *-ence*.

different | difference    evident | evidence    absent | absence

If the base word is a verb that ends in *ere*, remove the final *e* and add the suffix *-ence*.

revere | reverence    cohere | coherence    interfere | interference

| Base word | Word with suffix | Base word | Word with suffix |
| --- | --- | --- | --- |
| clear | | interfere | |
| excellent | | vary | |
| comply | | significant | |
| important | | confident | |
| adhere | | endure | |

2 Write a descriptive sentence using one of the words above with the suffix **-ence** or **-ance**.

_____

_____

_____

Now try this unit's 'Bringing it together' activity, which your teacher will give you.

**Phonology**

**1** Say each word and note which vowel phoneme it has. In the top row of the table, write the vowel phonemes you can hear. Then sort the words using the table. The first one is done for you.

| shed | threat | drip | straw | myth | dull | food | said | stalk |

| through | glove | force | sieve | blue | young | score | cleanse |

| screw | flood | launch | gym | realm | ridge | spruik | grudge |

| Short /e/ phoneme | _____ | _____ | _____ | _____ |
|---|---|---|---|---|
| shed | | | | |

**2** Complete the table below using the words from the last activity.

| | |
|---|---|
| All of the words with **/r/** as the second phoneme | |
| Three words that end with a consonant digraph | |
| All of the words with **/d/** as the third phoneme | |
| All of the words with the grapheme **y** representing a vowel | |
| The two words with the largest number of phonemes | |

OXFORD UNIVERSITY PRESS

**Orthography**

**1** There are a few ways to spell the **short /e/** phoneme (as in 'bed'). Read the sentences below the table. Some words have missing graphemes that represent the **short /e/** phoneme. Choose from the graphemes in the table to complete the words, then sort them using the table.

| Words with **e** | Words with **ea** | Words with **ai** |
|---|---|---|
| | | |

a   There was a **dr_____dful** smell emanating from the swamp.

b   The elephants were **b____llowing**.

c   Boomerangs and spears are examples of traditional hunting **w_____pons**.

d   My friend **s_____d** something that made me laugh.

e   An ____**thical** person is honest and has high moral standards.

f   My first **impr____ssion** of the artwork was that it was a photograph rather than a painting.

g   The carpenter needed to **m_____sure** the size of each room before starting the job.

h   The architect began to **sk____tch** a potential design for a new building.

i   Once **ag_____n**, it has started to rain.

j   The scientists' **br_____dth** of knowledge is admirable.

k   I struggled to carry the cumbersome **m____tal** toolbox.

l   Wild flowers can thrive in protected **m_____dows**.

m   We stood **ag_____nst** the brick wall while watching the parade.

**1** Use the base verbs listed in the tables on the next page to write sentences. Add the suffix listed in the table heading to the end of each base verb. The first one has been done for you.

Tip

Refer to page 13 if you need to review the rules for using the suffix **-s** or **-es**.

| Base verb | Sentence using base verb + suffix **-s** or **-es** |
|---|---|
| decide | When we play cricket, a flip of a coin <u>decides</u> who will bat first. |
| gain | |
| try | |
| experience | |
| push | |
| stop | |
| cover | |

Tip

Refer to pages 16–17 if you need to review the rules for using the suffix **-ing**.

| Base verb | Sentence using base verb + suffix **-ing** |
|---|---|
| decide | They gave up trying to cross the river, <u>deciding</u> that it wasn't worth the risk. |
| gain | |
| try | |
| experience | |

| Base verb | Sentence using base verb + suffix *-ing* |
|-----------|------------------------------------------|
| push      |                                          |
| stop      |                                          |
| cover     |                                          |

**Tip**

Refer to pages 24–25 if you need to review the rules for using the suffix *-ed*.

| Base verb | Sentence using base verb + suffix *-ed* |
|-----------|-----------------------------------------|
| decide    | Darren <u>decided</u> to stay home because he had a sore throat. |
| gain      |                                         |
| try       |                                         |
| experience|                                         |
| push      |                                         |
| stop      |                                         |
| cover     |                                         |

**Now try this unit's 'Bringing it together' activity, which your teacher will give you.**

**Phonology**

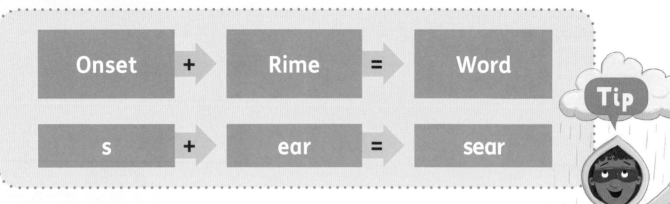

| Onset | + | Rime | = | Word |
|---|---|---|---|---|
| s | + | ear | = | sear |

**Tip**

**1** Sort these words using the table. Then add two more words with the same rime into each column.

| here | stair | star | fur | blur | stare |
|---|---|---|---|---|---|

| scar | stir | appear | galah | aware | hear |
|---|---|---|---|---|---|

| Words with the same rime as 'sear' | Words with the same rime as 'hair' | Words with the same rime as 'far' | Words with the same rime as 'her' |
|---|---|---|---|
| | | | |

**Orthography**

**1** There are several ways to spell the **/j/** phoneme, as in the word 'jam'. Read the sentences on the next page. Some words have missing letter patterns that involve the **/j/** phoneme. Choose from the letter patterns listed in the table on the next page to complete the words, then sort them using the table. You may use a dictionary to check the spelling of the words.

| Words with *dge* | Words with *dj* | Words with *ge* |
|---|---|---|
|  |  |  |

| Words with *gi* | Words with *gg* | Words with *j* |
|---|---|---|
|  |  |  |

a   When I spoke at assembly, I needed to **pro____ect** my voice.

b   There is a **smu_____** from the wet paint on my artwork.

c   The information was presented in a **lo____cal** manner.

d   To make the **oran_____** paint, mix the red and yellow together.

e   The meeting is **a_____ourned** until tomorrow.

f   The evidence **su_____ests** that most people enjoyed the movie.

g   The image on the front cover of the book did not do **____ustice** to the novel.

h   It is not helpful to hold a **gru_____** against a person.

i   My new **di_____tal** watch is more reliable than my old analogue watch.

j   Heart **sur_____ons** save many lives.

k   A **____ournalist** is a person who prepares news stories to be published or broadcast.

l   Aboriginal and Torres Strait Islander cultures developed over countless **_____nerations**.

m   I had difficulty **a_____usting** my seatbelt.

n   They will **dre_____** the river to allow larger vessels to travel along it.

o   I think my teacher was **exa_____erating** when she said how difficult the test would be.

p   The castle kitchen **a_____oins** a large courtyard.

q   We spent the afternoon exploring the quaint French **villa_____** .

**Tip**

A plural noun is a word that tells us that there is more than one thing. 'Icicles' and 'gorillas' are plural nouns.

The suffix **-s** or **-es** can be added to many nouns to create plural nouns.

**1** Use the rules to complete the sentences. Then find another word that follows each rule, and use it in a new sentence. You can scan a book you are reading to find suitable words.

**If a base word ends in s, x, z, ch or sh, add the suffix -es.**

| Base word | Sentence |
|---|---|
| speech | Three funny _____ entertained us during the assembly. |
|  |  |

**If a base word ends in f or fe, it is usual to change the f or fe to a v and then add the suffix -es.**

| Base word | Sentence |
|---|---|
| elf | Mythical creatures known as _____ derive from folklore. |
|  |  |

**If a base word ends in a vowel and the letter o, add the suffix -s.**

| Base word | Sentence |
|---|---|
| cameo | _____ are small oval-shaped brooches with a carved portrait. |
|  |  |

| Base word | Sentence |
|---|---|
| bridge | Several of the ancient _____ need to be restored. |

| Base word | Sentence |
|---|---|
| mosquito | The riverbank is a breeding ground for _____. |

| Base word | Sentence |
|---|---|
| hobby | My favourite _____ are painting and cooking. |

Now try this unit's 'Bringing it together' activity, which your teacher will give you.

# UNIT 12

Phonology

**1** Say each word and sort them using the table. Then find some more words with these phonemes in a book you are reading and add them to the table.

| fragrant | thorough | nervous | breathe | different | worthy |

| evaporate | massively | phenomena | whether | thermometer | birthday |

| Words with a **/f/** phoneme | Words with a **/v/** phoneme |
|---|---|
|  |  |

| Words with an unvoiced **/th/** phoneme, as in 'thing' | Words with a voiced **/th/** phoneme, as in 'that' |
|---|---|
|  |  |

OXFORD UNIVERSITY PRESS

**Tip**

A vowel letter usually follows the phoneme **/v/** in a word. If a word ends with **/v/**, the letters **ve** are used as a digraph. The word 'of' is an exception.

1　The words below are incomplete. Decide whether to use **va**, **ve**, **vi**, **vo** or **vu** to complete them. You may use a dictionary to check the spelling of the words.

_____cating        appro_____        in_____tation        _____lcano        con_____lse

cur_____        _____luntary        ad_____nce        achie_____        indi_____dual

_____sible        _____lture        carni_____l        _____lnerable        creati_____

ine_____table        _____yage        e_____luate        a_____cado

Underline the words above that end with the **/v/** phoneme.
Circle the words with the **ve** digraph.

2　Read aloud from a book you are reading. See if you can find some words with the **/v/** phoneme. Copy five of these words into the table below and underline the letter **v** and the vowel letter that follows it. Then copy the sentence you found it in.

| Word with the **/v/** phoneme | Sentence |
| --- | --- |
| | |

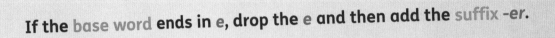

**Tip**

The suffix **-er** can be used to change a base verb to a person noun. For example, the verb 'dance' can be changed to the noun 'dancer' – someone who dances.

**1** Use the rules to complete the tables. Make sure that each word you choose follows the same rule as the example.

**If the base word ends in e, drop the e and then add the suffix -er.**

| Verb | Person noun with **-er** suffix | Sentence |
|---|---|---|
| compose | composer | Wolfgang Amadeus Mozart was a famous <u>composer</u>. |
| | | |
| | | |

**If the base word ends with a short vowel graph then a consonant graph other than x, double the last letter and then add the suffix -er.**

| Verb | Person noun with **-er** suffix | Sentence |
|---|---|---|
| drum | drummer | The band has a singer, two guitarists and a <u>drummer</u>. |
| | | |
| | | |

Now try this unit's 'Bringing it together' activity, which your teacher will give you.

# UNIT 13

**1** Say each word. Sort the words using the table.

| account | annoy | decay | portrayal | thousand | disappointing |

| voyage | pounding | drainage | choice | empowering | payment |

| Words with the **/ow/** phoneme, as in 'now' | Words with the **/oi/** phoneme, as in 'soy' | Words with the **long /a/** phoneme, as in 'prey' |
| --- | --- | --- |
| | | |

**2** Remember that the **/ow/**, **/oi/** and **long /a/** phonemes are all diphthongs. The following words have **/ow/** (as in 'cow' and 'sound'), **/oi/** (as in 'alloy' and 'coin') or **long /a/** (as in 'say' and 'rain').

Decide which version of the word is spelled correctly, circle it and read it aloud, then write it on the line provided. Underline the letters that represent the diphthong in each word you write. You may use a dictionary to check your answers.

a    mointainous    mountainous    maintainous    _____

b    betrayal    betrowl    betroyl    _____

c    powder    poyder    payder    _____

d    araind    aroind    around    _____

e    retown    retoin    retain    _____

f    enjayment    enjowment    enjoyment    _____

g    poisonous    paysoinous    powsonous    _____

**1** Read the sentences. Some words have missing letters that represent the diphthong **/ow/**, as in 'cow'. Write either **ow** or **ou** to complete the words.

a   Tibet is one of the most **m_____ntainous** places in the world.

b   It is unlikely that a **p_____er** station will be built in this area.

c   It can be a challenge to **pron_____nce** foreign words.

d   A famous botanist **enc_____ntered** a new plant.

e   The garden is blooming with **fl_____ers** of all varieties.

f   Members of the local **c_____ncil** meet once a month.

g   Josef was feeling **d_____btful** that he would win.

h   I felt **dr_____sy** after the long journey.

**2** Scan a book you are reading. Find some more words with **ou** or **ow** representing the diphthong **/ow/**. Write them in the table.

| Words with **ou** | Words with **ow** |
| --- | --- |
|  |  |

**3** Read the sentences. Some words have missing letters that represent the diphthong **/oi/**, as in 'boy'. Write either **oy** or **oi** to complete the words.

a   Matilda counted her collection of **c_____ns**.

b   The new company will provide **empl_____ment** for many people.

c   Sudden **n_____ses** can frighten my dog.

d   The leader inspires **l_____alty** in the community.

e   The word 'fun' starts with an **unv_____ced** phoneme.

f   A person who is **flamb_____ant** attracts attention because of their vibrant personality.

g   My dentist **app_____ntment** is scheduled for tomorrow afternoon.

h   The potter added water to **m_____sten** the clay.

**4** Scan a book you are reading. Find some more words with **oi** or **oy** representing the diphthong **/oi/**. Write them in the table.

| Words with **oi** | Words with **oy** |
| --- | --- |
| | |
| | |

**1** Use the homophones to complete the sentences. You may use a dictionary to help you.

flower/flour        foul/fowl

**a**   A hen is a type of _____.

**b**   Two essential ingredients needed to make pasta are _____ and eggs.

**c**   The odour of rotten eggs is _____.

**d**   Adding a frangipani _____ to the roses will make the room smell beautiful.

**2** Write your own sentences using the homophones.

| flower | |
| --- | --- |
| flour | |
| foul | |
| fowl | |

**Now try this unit's 'Bringing it together' activity, which your teacher will give you.**

**Phonology**

**1** Read the multisyllabic words in the table. In the next column, write which phoneme is a schwa. Then write down more multisyllabic words with a schwa from a book you are reading. Notice that some multisyllabic words do not have a schwa.

| Multisyllabic word | Position of schwa | Multisyllabic word in texts I am reading | Position of schwa |
|---|---|---|---|
| company | 5th phoneme | | |
| important | | | |
| national | | | |
| probably | | | |
| politics | | | |
| managing | | | |
| causation | | | |
| imposter | | | |
| necessary | | | |
| broccoli | | | |

**Orthography**

**1** There are many ways to spell the **/aw/** phoneme, as in 'chalk'. The words below have missing letters that involve the **/aw/** phoneme. Choose from the letter patterns in the table on the next page to complete the words, then write the completed words in the table.

Use a dictionary to check the spelling if you are not sure.

OXFORD UNIVERSITY PRESS

abn_____mality    w_____ nuts    ad_____    h_____k    astron_____t

keyb_____d    rew_____ding    gal_____    outd_____s    m_____nful

br_____t    withdr_____    th_____tful    abs_____ption    inst_____

p_____sing    ab_____d    tow_____ds    t_____naments    p_____ly

| or |
| --- |
| aw |
| au |
| al or all |
| ar |
| oar |
| oor |
| ore |
| our |
| ough |

**1** Use the homophones to complete the sentences. You may use a dictionary if you are not sure.

serial/cereal     cymbal/symbol

**a** We asked the drummer to play the crash _____ more quietly.

**b** I added some yoghurt and fruit to my breakfast _____ .

**c** A large biohazard _____ was displayed on the steel drum.

**d** My favourite _____ stories are science fiction.

**2** Write your own sentences using the homophones.

| serial | |
| --- | --- |
| cereal | |
| cymbal | |
| symbol | |

Now try this unit's 'Bringing it together' activity, which your teacher will give you.

# UNIT 15

**1** These words have an r-influenced vowel phoneme. Sort the words using the table.

| startle | nervous | heritage | research | careless | scar | argument |
|---------|---------|----------|----------|----------|------|----------|

| pleasurable | preparing | artist | journey | awareness |
|-------------|-----------|--------|---------|-----------|

| sharpen | reoccur | deserve | declare | archive |
|---------|---------|---------|---------|---------|

| firmly | adverb | journal | repaired | carving |
|--------|--------|---------|----------|---------|

| unfairly | billionaire | embark | glares | bizarre |
|----------|-------------|--------|--------|---------|

| Words with **/er/**, as in 'stir' | Words with **/air/**, as in 'rare' | Words with **/ar/**, as in 'lark' |
|---|---|---|
| | | |

> **Tip**
>
> Sometimes r-influenced vowel phonemes can sound a little different, depending on the way a person pronounces them. Sometimes they can sound like a schwa, an **/uh/** sound, but the spelling doesn't change.

**1** There are many ways to spell the **/er/** phoneme (as in 'her'). The words below have missing letters that represent the **/er/** phoneme. Choose from the graphemes in the table below to complete each word, then sort the words using the table.

**Tip**

Use a dictionary to check the spelling of the words if you are not sure.

aff_____m          res_____ching     st_____dy       inj_____s       adv_____bial

w_____kable        medioc_____        adj_____n     kilomet_____s     f_____mly

_____thquake       obs_____ve          flav_____less  pict_____s      occ_____red

w_____thy          g_____m             ch_____ning     st_____           y_____n

conj_____s       w_____ship          sav_____y     fib_____s

| *ir* | *er* | *ear* | *ur* |
| --- | --- | --- | --- |
| | | | |

| *ure* | *or* | *our* | *re* |
| --- | --- | --- | --- |
| | | | |

OXFORD UNIVERSITY PRESS

**1** Use the homophones to complete the sentences.
You may use a dictionary to help you.

| earn/urn | birth/berth |
| --- | --- |

**a** The cruise ship will _____
at the pier tomorrow.

**b** A large container that heats water is called an

_____ .

**c** Jade will _____ some
pocket money if she mows her neighbour's lawn.

**d** There is a higher _____ rate in the city.

**2** Write your own sentences using the homophones.

| earn | |
| --- | --- |
| urn | |
| birth | |
| berth | |

Now try
this unit's 'Bringing
it together' activity,
which your teacher
will give you.

OXFORD UNIVERSITY PRESS

**1** The words below have an r-influenced vowel phoneme. Sort the words using the table.

| fearful | disheartening | circus | heritage | mournful | endearing |

| reward | stirring | charming | harshest | cavalier | warehouse |

| awareness | purple | bursting | orthography | enforce | serial |

| parsnip | disrepair | heard | gourmet | volunteer | carpet | dairy |

| | |
|---|---|
| Words with **/ear/**, as in 'near' | |
| Words with **/ar/**, as in 'start' | |
| Words with **/air/**, as in 'pear' | |
| Words with **/er/**, as in 'learn' | |
| Words with **/aw/**, as in 'talk' | |

**2** Find some more words with these r-influenced vowel phonemes in a book you are reading and add them to the table.

**Tip**

If you are reading a book from North America, you might notice some spelling differences. The final phoneme in words such as 'colour' and 'favour' is spelled **or** instead of **our**.

**1** There are many ways to spell the **/k/** phoneme (as in 'kite'). The words below have missing letters that represent the **/k/** phoneme. Choose from the graphemes in the table below to complete each word, then sort the words using the table.

**Tip**

Use a dictionary to check the spelling of these words if you are not sure.

____olourful

breathta____ing

ara_____nid

shipwre_____

uni_____ly

mar____ets

chi_____en

opa_____

monar_____y

re____ommend

grotes_____

bro____en

pa_____age

s____raping

_____aotic

_____oir

obli_____

wi_____ed

____itten

a____tivities

| c |
|---|
| k |
| ck |
| ch |
| que |

**2** Choose one word from each row of the table and write a sentence that uses all of your chosen words. You may add suffixes to the words if you need to. Then circle those words.

_____

_____

_____

The suffixes **-able** and **-ible** mean 'able to be' or 'worthy of'. They can be added to the end of some base words to form adjectives, such as 'enjoyable' (able to be enjoyed).

The suffix **-able** is more common than the suffix **-ible**.

The suffix **-able** is generally used when a complete word comes before it (e.g. 'laugh' becomes 'laughable'). It is common to use **-ible** after a word ending in the **/s/** phoneme (e.g. 'sense' becomes 'sensible'). The suffix **-ible** is also often used after an incomplete word.

**1** Complete the table by adding the suffix **-able** to each base word and using it in a sentence. Underline the adjective with the suffix in each sentence. The first one is done for you.

| Base word | Sentence |
|---|---|
| reason | The cost of the new car is <u>reasonable</u>. |
| manage | |
| comfort | |
| sustain | |

**2** The adjectives below end with the suffix **-ible**. Underline the suffix **-ible** in each word. Write the matching base word. Then write a sentence using the adjective. The first one is done for you.

**If the base word ends in e, usually drop the e before adding the suffix -ible.**

| Adjective | Base word | Sentence |
|---|---|---|
| revers<u>ible</u> | reverse | I wore my new <u>reversible</u> jacket on the weekend. |
| collapsible | | |
| responsible | | |

**3** Read the list of adjectives. These words also end in **-ible** but the letters that come before the suffix do not make a complete word on their own. Circle the suffix in each adjective and underline the part of the word that comes before the suffix. Then write a sentence using the adjective. The first one is done for you.

| Adjective with suffix | Sentence |
|---|---|
| neglig(ible) | The difference in taste between the two cakes is negligible. |
| tangible | |
| legible | |
| plausible | |

**Tip**

Etymology is the study of where words come from and how they have changed over time.

**4** Use an online etymology dictionary to find out the origin of the words listed in the table below. Write a definition for each word.

**Tip**

Notice that the **que** in these words represents the **/k/** phoneme.

| Word | Origin | Definition |
|---|---|---|
| grotesque | | |
| picturesque | | |
| technique | | |

Now try this unit's 'Bringing it together' activity, which your teacher will give you.

**1** Each word below has a consonant blend. It might be an initial consonant blend (at the start of a word); a medial one (in the middle of a word); or a final one (at the end of a word). Sort the words using the table. Then underline the consonant blend in each word.

chlorine   ginger   revamp   silent   spelling   doctor   gender   evict

spirit   create   cobra   demand   reject   sample   bamboo   suggest

closure   against   surround   private   master   scratches   adopt

slither   employ   nuclear   frozen   stamina   detect   central

| Initial consonant blend | Medial consonant blend | Final consonant blend |
|---|---|---|
| | | |

OXFORD UNIVERSITY PRESS

**1** Read the sentences. Some words have missing letters that represent the **long /a/** phoneme (as in 'made'). Choose from the graphemes to complete each word.

| ay | ai | a-e | eigh | a | ae | ey | ei | ea | et | ée |

a   The once beautiful village had fallen into a state of **dec_____**.

b   That was the **gr_____test** movie I have ever seen.

c   The **accl_____med** professor published a new report.

d   Our dog was feeling unwell so we checked her **w_____t**.

e   The football **st___dium** was packed for the grand final.

f   The **soir_____** was attended by the wealthiest patrons of the city.

g   The prime minister was asked to make a **st___t___ment** about the upcoming election.

h   My Irish grandmother is fluent in **G_____lic**.

i   The graph **conv_____s** the data in a succinct manner.

j   Eating a balanced diet helps your body to **obt_____n** the nutrients it needs.

k   If you don't read those books, they may **accumul___t___** dust.

l   The security company claimed that the window was **unbr_____kable**.

m   The markets have a massive **arr_____** of spices from around the world.

n   The restaurant specialises in **gourm_____** French cuisine.

o   We were fortunate to relocate to a lovely **n_____bourhood**.

p   We ordered a plate of calamari as an **entr_____**.

q   The earthquake could be felt in a five-hundred-kilometre **r____dius**.

r   The compost was filled with insect **larv_____**.

s   The **ball_____** dancers performed gracefully.

t   The government conducted a **surv_____** on languages spoken at home.

u   Arteries carry blood away from the heart and **v_____ns** carry blood back to it.

v   He painted the tea cups blue and **b_____ge**.

**2** Sort the words you completed in the last activity using the table below and on the next page.

| ay | |
| --- | --- |
| ai | |
| a-e | |
| eigh | |

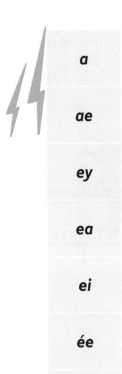

| a |
| --- |
| ae |
| ey |
| ea |
| ei |
| ée |
| et |

The suffixes **-hood**, **-ship** and **-dom** can be used to form nouns. The new word means something like the condition of being of the base word.

For instance, 'motherhood' means the condition of being a mother and 'companionship' means the condition of being companions.

Words created with the suffix **-dom** can also mean the area in which something operates, such as 'kingdom', which is a country that is ruled by a king or a queen.

**1** Make nouns from the base words by adding the suffixes **-hood**, **-ship** or **-dom**. You may use a dictionary to help you.

Dictionary

| Base word | Noun with suffix | Base word | Noun with suffix |
| --- | --- | --- | --- |
| child | | relation | |
| friend | | bore | |
| sponsor | | member | |

| Base word | Noun with suffix | Base word | Noun with suffix |
|-----------|------------------|-----------|------------------|
| king | | adult | |
| champion | | neighbour | |
| free | | leader | |

**Tip**

English has borrowed many words from other languages and they often have letter patterns that are different from those found in English. For example, the grapheme **ée** can be found in some French words that are now used in English, such as the word 'matinée'.

The symbol above the first **e** in 'matinée' is called an acute accent.

2   Use an online etymology dictionary to find out the origin of the words in the table below. Write a definition for each word.

| Word | Origin | Definition |
|------|--------|------------|
| soirée | | |
| toupee | | |
| rendezvous | | |
| ballet | | |
| protégé | | |

Now try this unit's 'Bringing it together' activity, which your teacher will give you.

**1** Each word below has a consonant digraph. It might be an initial consonant digraph (at the start of a word); a medial one (in the middle of a word); or a final one (at the end of a word). Sort the words using the table and underline the consonant digraph in each word.

| carries | perish | chlorinated | bonding | socket | effect |
| charmer | thousand | wrinkle | washable | lavish | careless |
| unleash | shoulders | narrow | torrent | fortress | sheltered |
| reaches | column | vanish | champion | chemist | machines |
| express | slither | threaten | beneath | support | thermostat |

| Initial consonant digraph | Medial consonant digraph | Final consonant digraph |
| --- | --- | --- |
| | | |

OXFORD UNIVERSITY PRESS

**1** Read the sentences. Some words have missing letters that represent the **long /e/** phoneme (as in 'street'). Choose from the graphemes to complete each word. You may use a dictionary to check the spelling of the words.

| ee | ea | e | e-e | ie | ei |
|---|---|---|---|---|---|

a   My favourite actor will **f_____ture** in the new film.

b   It is normal for toddlers to display **____gocentric** behaviour.

c   Toby rolled the ball **betw_____n** two desks.

d   Industrial agriculture can **depl___t___** soil fertility.

e   A **dec_____tful** person can be untrustworthy as they tend to lie.

f   The tractor has a **d_____sel** engine.

g   If you wish to **succ_____d**, you should persist with challenging tasks.

h   People can do amazing things when they **bel_____ve** in the power of their dreams.

i   Please divide the pie into four **___qual** parts.

j   A quiet forest is more **ser___n___** than a crowded beach.

k   I will **s_____ze** the opportunity to visit an ancient castle.

l   It is **r_____sonable** to expect hotter days during the summer months.

**2** Sort the words you completed in the last activity using the table.

| ee | |
|---|---|
| ea | |
| e | |
| e-e | |
| ie | |
| ei | |

**1** Use the homophones to complete the sentences. You may use a dictionary to help you.

| peak/peek | steel/steal | piece/peace |
| --- | --- | --- |

**a** The hikers climbed to the _____ of the tallest mountain.

**b** A common material used for the construction of car bodies is _____ .

**c** I like to _____ out of the window.

**d** There is a sense of _____ and calm among the people.

**e** I placed a generous _____ of meat on my plate.

**f** It is against the law to _____ from other people.

**2** Write your own sentences using the homophones.

| peak | |
| --- | --- |
| peek | |
| steel | |
| steal | |
| piece | |
| peace | |

OXFORD UNIVERSITY PRESS

A mnemonic is a strategy to help you remember something.

The sentence 'Have a *piece* of *pie*' will help you remember the spelling of 'piece'.

**3** Select two homophones that you sometimes misspell. Create a mnemonic to help you remember the spelling of each homophone.

a _____

_____

_____

b _____

_____

_____

**4** Now use a homophone you wrote about in the last activity in a sentence.

_____

_____

Now try this unit's 'Bringing it together' activity, which your teacher will give you.

# UNIT 19

**1** Sort the words using the table.

| misunderstood | exotic | bamboozle | willow | bellowing | soothing |

| trophy | province | nonsense | cookware | approachable | pollen | solemn |

| driftwood | droopy | hoodwink | harpoon | cocoon | cyclone | couldn't |

| | |
|---|---|
| Words with a **short /oo/**, as in 'should' | |
| Words with a **long /oo/**, as in 'lute' | |
| Words with a **short /o/**, as in 'what' | |
| Words with a **long /o/**, as in 'show' | |

**2** Scan a book you are reading to find some more words with these vowel phonemes. Write the sentences you found these words in. Then underline the words with the **short /oo/**, **long /oo/**, **short /o/** or **long /o/** phonemes in the sentences you wrote.

| Phoneme | Sentence |
|---|---|
| **short /oo/** as in 'took' | |

| Phoneme | Sentence |
|---|---|
| **long /oo/** as in 'soon' | |
| **short /o/** as in 'hot' | |
| **long /o/** as in 'flow' | |
| Phoneme | Sentence |

OXFORD UNIVERSITY PRESS

**1** Read the sentences. Some words have missing letters that represent the **long /o/** phoneme (as in 'know'). Choose from the graphemes to complete the words. You may use a dictionary to check the spelling of the words.

| ow | oa | o-e | o | oe | ough | eau |

a I will be **borr_____ing** some books from the school library tomorrow.

b A person who is **b_____stful** is overly proud of something they can do.

c In drama, my teacher asked me to **ev___k___** the feeling of excitement in my character.

d An **avocad___** is a fruit that is high in monounsaturated fatty acids.

e The heroine travelled across the great land to confront her **f_____**.

f **Alth_____** the campsite was far away, the smell of the barbecue was alluring.

g The weather **bur_____** predicts a snowstorm in the coming days.

h My fingers and **t_____s** feel numb because the weather is so cold.

i Let's sit under the shade of the **will_____** tree.

j In France, we visited an opulent **chat_____**.

k I decided not to go to the show even **th_____** I won a ticket.

l Our new school principal is friendly and **appr_____chable**.

m My preparation for the athletics carnival was **medi___cre** as I wasn't feeling well.

n A massive tropical **cycl___n___** devastated the city of Darwin in 1974.

**2** Sort the words you completed in the last activity using the table below and on the next page.

| ow | |
|---|---|
| **oa** | |
| **o-e** | |
| **o** | |
| **oe** | |

OXFORD UNIVERSITY PRESS

*ough*

*eau*

**1** Use the homophones to complete the sentences.
You may use a dictionary to help you.

groan/grown    draft/draught

**a** I revised the first _____ of my
story after I got feedback from my teacher.

**b** The chef let out a _____ when he realised the roast
was burnt.

**c** A _____ of cool air could be felt in every room.

**d** The wheat crop has _____ quickly this season.

**2** Write your own sentences using the homophones.

| | |
|---|---|
| groan | |
| grown | |
| draft | |
| draught | |

Now try this unit's 'Bringing
it together' activity, which your
teacher will give you.

**Phonology**

## The Glimme
### by Emily Rodda

Everyone looked around, thunderstruck. A tall woman was standing at the entrance to the yard. Tinted glasses masked her eyes and gloves covered her hands. Behind her was a fine carriage drawn by a sweating horse that shivered and pawed the ground. A sullen man crouched on the driver's seat, holding tightly to the reins.

**1** Read the text above and find words in it to complete the table.

| | |
|---|---|
| All one-syllable words ending in **ed** | |
| A disyllabic word starting with a consonant digraph | |
| Four disyllabic words starting with a consonant blend | |
| Two multisyllabic words starting with the same vowel phoneme | |
| A three-syllable word | |

| Three disyllabic words with a consonant digraph at the syllable juncture | |
|---|---|
| Three words with five phonemes | |
| Three words with six phonemes | |
| Two words with seven phonemes | |
| All disyllabic words with a **long /i/** phoneme | |
| All words with an **/ow/** diphthong | |

| A word that ... | |
|---|---|
| has ten phonemes | |
| rhymes with 'gains' | |
| rhymes with 'brightly' | |
| has an unvoiced **/th/** phoneme | |
| ends with an accented syllable | |
| has a schwa as the fourth phoneme | |

**1** Read the sentences. Some words have missing letters that represent the **long /oo/** phoneme (as in 'moon'). Choose from the graphemes to complete each word. You may use a dictionary to check the spelling of the words.

| ue | oo | u-e | ew | ou | u | ui | o | ough |
|----|----|----|----|----|----|----|----|----|

a   I find it easier to get my work done when I am in a good **r_____tine**.

b   We walked **thr_____** the rainforest.

c   I looked under my bed and found the **gr_____some** remains of an old sandwich.

d   The Crown **J_____els** can be viewed in the Tower of London.

e   Our meeting was **fr_____tful**, in that we made some important decisions.

f   Performing well in the competition has given me a **b_____st** of confidence.

g   We can **dil___t___** the lemon juice by adding some water.

h   I wonder **wh___** the special visitor will be at the next assembly.

i   The aristocrat showed off her **r___by** ring to the dinner party guests.

j   It was a dark and **gl_____my** morning.

k   The tram is a **s_____table** form of transport.

l   A new **s_____age** treatment plant was constructed for the town.

m   I was given one **cl_____** to help me figure out the puzzle.

n   It's **cr___cial** that hikers check for weather warnings before ascending the peak.

o   I will **concl___d___** my speech by telling a joke.

p   We thought that the new action **m___vie** was outstanding.

q   Our mother told us about going camping every summer in her **y_____th**.

r   **Thr_____out** the summer holidays, the parks were really busy.

**2** Sort the words you completed in the last activity using the table below and on the next page.

| ue |  |
|----|----|
| oo |  |
| u-e |  |
| ew |  |
| ou |  |

OXFORD UNIVERSITY PRESS

| u |
|---|
| ui |
| o |
| ough |

**1** Use the homophones to complete the sentences.
You may use a dictionary to help you.

| muscles/mussels | residents/residence |
|---|---|

**a** The queen is spending August in her summer _____.

**b** In some freshwater and saltwater habitats, _____,
a type of mollusc, can be found.

**c** The human body has hundreds of _____.

**d** More than fifty _____ live in the block
of apartments.

**2** Write your own sentences using the homophones.

| muscles | |
|---|---|
| mussels | |
| residents | |
| residence | |

**Now try this unit's 'Bringing it together'
activity, which your teacher will give you.**

**1** Sort these words using the table.

| bonsai | chief | tomb | vital | receive | egocentric |

| sewage | delight | reasonable | crucial | movie |

| scientific | machinery | resolute | ceiling | soup |

| extreme | client | monsoonal | grind | pesticide |

| Words with a **long /e/**, as in 'need' | Words with a **long /i/**, as in 'side' | Words with a **long /oo/**, as in 'moon' |
|---|---|---|
|  |  |  |

**2** Scan a book you are reading to find some more words with these vowel phonemes. Add the words to the table above.

**1** Read the sentences. Some words have missing letters that represent the **long /i/** phoneme (as in 'side'). Choose from the graphemes to complete each word.

| igh | y | i-e | ie | i | ai | ei |
|-----|---|-----|----|----|----|----|

a    The well-known Japanese poet Matsuo Basho is famous for his **h_____ku** poems.

b    The heritage society has a photographic **arch___v___** of the city's earliest buildings.

c    The online documentary offers **ins_____tful** information on space junk.

d    A **s___napse** is the gap between two neurons in the brain.

e    I was disappointed to learn that my friend told a **l_____**.

f    The photographic artwork featured a **kal_____doscope** of vivid colours.

g    The **cl___max** of the movie was amplified by intense sound effects.

h    Receiving a bouquet of flowers was a **del_____tful** surprise.

i    The technique known as **bons_____** produces miniature plants that mimic large trees.

j    A measure of **s_____smic** waves determines the amplitude of an earthquake.

k    It's important to wash the fruit because it has been sprayed with **pestic___d___**.

l    Although **p___thons** are not venomous, they can bite or constrict.

m    The shopkeeper was busy attending to many **cl_____ents**.

n    The Australian **magp_____** is a black and white bird with a beautiful voice.

**2** Sort the words you completed in the last activity using the table.

| igh | |
|-----|---|
| y | |
| i-e | |
| ie | |
| i | |
| ai | |
| ei | |

**1** Use the homophones 'wail', 'whale', 'lapse' and 'laps', to complete the sentences. You may use a dictionary to help you.

**a** My tennis club membership will _____ if I don't renew it soon.

**b** An example of a mammal that lives in the ocean is the humpback _____.

**c** My little sister started to _____ when she fell off her bike.

**d** The swimmer swam ten _____ of the pool in record time.

**2** Write your own sentences using the homophones.

| | |
|---|---|
| wail | |
| whale | |
| laps | |
| lapse | |

> **Tip**
>
> A morpheme is the smallest chunk of meaning in a word. For instance, the word 'powerful' has two morphemes, the base word 'power' and the suffix **-ful**.
>
> A free morpheme is a complete word, such as 'graph' in the word 'hydrograph'.
>
> A bound morpheme isn't a word on its own, such as **hydro** in the word 'hydrograph'.

**3** The Greek morpheme **hydro** means 'water'. Add the morpheme **hydro** to complete each word in the first column of the table. Then write a definition for each word, using a dictionary to help you. The first one is done for you.

| | |
|---|---|
| **hydro**logy | The scientific study of water |
| _____graphy | |
| _____gen | |
| _____power | |

OXFORD UNIVERSITY PRESS

Many words end with more than one suffix. The word 'beautifully' has the suffix **-ful** followed by the suffix **-ly**.

**4** The word 'hydrograph' is made up of two morphemes. Use the suffixes to make new words starting with 'hydrograph'. You may use a dictionary to help you.

| Suffixes | -al | -er | -ic | -ly | -s | -y |
|---|---|---|---|---|---|---|
| Words starting with 'hydrograph': | | | | | | |

**5** The Latin morpheme **aqua** also means 'water'. Add the morpheme **aqua** to complete each word in the first column of the table. Then write each whole word in a sentence, using a dictionary to help you.

| **aqua**rium | The aquarium is home to over 400 species of sea creatures. |
|---|---|
| _____tic | |
| _____marine | |
| _____plane | |

Now try this unit's 'Bringing it together' activity, which your teacher will give you.

## Phonology

**1** Say each disyllabic word. Notice that each word has an accented syllable and an unaccented syllable. Sort the words using the table.

| technique | image | sequence | display | express |

| figure | describe | engrave | opaque | neutral |

| First syllable is accented | Second syllable is accented |
| --- | --- |
| | |

**2** Find four more disyllabic words from a subject you're studying, such as maths, music or art. Add the words to the table above.

## Orthography

**1** Read the sentences below and on the next page. Some words have missing letters that represent the last two phonemes. Choose from the letter patterns to complete the words. You may use a dictionary to check your spelling.

**al**          **el**          **le**

a   A **cam**_____ can travel in the desert for long periods without water.

b   Engineers are investigating where the leak in the **tunn**_____ is coming from.

c   The injured **anim**_____ was treated by the vet.

d   We went to the **loc**_____ swimming pool on the first day of the holidays.

e   My family is planning to **trav**_____ overseas next year.

f   At the festival, there was a large gathering of **peop**_____ from many cultures.

OXFORD UNIVERSITY PRESS

**g** Heading towards the mouth of the river, we paddled our canoe on the **chann_____** .

**h** The stunning **cor_____** reef is home to thousands of tropical fish.

**i** The glass **bott_____** is filled with sparkling water.

**j** Quartz is a **cryst_____** that has many uses.

**k** Heat can trigger a **chemic_____** reaction.

**l** I stood in a puddle of water that was **ank_____** deep.

**m** An interesting **artic_____** about viruses was published today.

**n** I will **sprink_____** some nuts and seeds on my salad to add protein.

**o** To get to the dog park, you need to walk down the **grav_____** track.

**2** Use the table below to sort the words you completed in the last activity.

| | |
|---|---|
| *al* | |
| *el* | |
| *le* | |

> **Tip**
>
> The letter pattern **le** is found at the end of words, such as 'people' and 'article'. Usually, this letter pattern does not appear after the letters **m**, **n**, **r**, **v** or **w**.

**3** Scan some books you are reading to find some base words ending in **le**. Look at the letter pattern that comes before the **le** in these words. Complete the table with the words you've found, using the examples to help you.

| ending in **ble** | ending in **cle** | ending in **kle** | ending in **dle** | ending in **gle** |
|---|---|---|---|---|
| ta**ble** | cir**cle** | spar**kle** | mid**dle** | strug**gle** |

| ending in **fle** | ending in **ple** | ending in **tle** | ending in **stle** | ending in **zle** |
|---|---|---|---|---|
| sti**fle** | ap**ple** | tur**tle** | whi**stle** | puz**zle** |

**Tip**

The suffix **-ism** can be added to a word to represent a practice, system or belief. For instance, the word 'Buddhism' refers to the belief system of people who follow the teachings of Buddha, a teacher, philosopher and spiritual leader from Ancient India.

**1** Use a dictionary to find out the meaning of these words with the suffix **-ism**. Write a descriptive sentence using each word.

| Word | Sentence |
|---|---|
| tourism | |
| journalism | |
| criticism | |
| impressionism | |
| cynicism | |
| nationalism | |
| realism | |
| capitalism | |

**2** The Latin morpheme **audi** means 'hearing', 'listening' or 'sound'. Add the morpheme **audi** to complete each word in the first column of the table. Then write a definition for each word, using a dictionary to help you. The first one is done for you.

| Word starting with **audi** | Definition |
|---|---|
| <u>audi</u>ble | Able to be heard |
| _____torium | |
| _____ology | |

OXFORD UNIVERSITY PRESS

**3** The Latin morpheme **ben** means 'good'. Use this morpheme to complete the table below.

| Word starting with **ben** | Definition |
| --- | --- |
| <u>ben</u>efit | An advantage gained from something |
| _____efactor | |
| _____ign | |

**4** The Latin morpheme **cent** means 'hundred'. Use this morpheme to complete the table below.

| Word starting with **cent** | Definition |
| --- | --- |
| <u>cent</u>enary | A hundredth anniversary |
| _____ury | |
| _____ipede | |

**5** The Latin morpheme **circum** means 'around'. Use this morpheme to complete the table below.

| Words starting with **circum** | Definition |
| --- | --- |
| <u>circum</u>ference | The enclosed boundary of a circular shape |
| _____stance | |
| _____spect | |

Now try this unit's 'Bringing it together' activity, which your teacher will give you.

# UNIT 23

**1** The words below are missing one of these five initial consonant blends:

| shr | scr | str | spl | spr |
|-----|-----|-----|-----|-----|

Complete the words using the blends. You may use a dictionary to check your answers.

_____utinise     _____endid     _____inkage     _____inkles     _____unch

_____atosphere     _____ubbery     _____enuous     _____intery     _____ounge

_____outing     _____eakiest     _____ucture     _____ingent     _____ink

_____uttered     _____ibble     _____urge     _____eadsheet

**1** The words below have some missing letters. The missing letters represent an r-influenced vowel phoneme that can be heard in the unaccented final syllable of many words, such as 'theatre' and 'calendar'. Choose from the graphemes **or**, **our**, **er** and **ar** to complete the words. You may use a dictionary to check your spelling.

endeav_____     eag_____     monit_____     vineg_____

foy_____     mirr_____     neighb_____     gramm_____

nucle_____     daught_____     doct_____     flav_____

**2** Choose one word with each grapheme from the last activity. Write a descriptive sentence for each of the words.

| Grapheme | Descriptive sentence including a word with this grapheme |
|----------|----------------------------------------------------------|
| **ar** | |
| **er** | |
| **or** | |
| **our** | |

OXFORD UNIVERSITY PRESS

**3** Find these words in the word search.

| b | s | e | d | q | p | y | e | z | u | w | k | w | m | u |
|---|---|---|---|---|---|---|---|---|---|---|---|---|---|---|
| s | m | u | n | z | g | f | c | v | v | s | p | z | i | f |
| x | d | c | g | h | b | u | p | x | m | k | c | c | h | g |
| j | f | r | d | a | q | w | i | j | e | p | k | r | t | n |
| h | v | o | n | d | r | a | q | t | t | x | b | i | a | e |
| a | l | l | i | g | a | t | o | r | a | e | i | g | h | j |
| f | o | s | a | v | o | u | r | s | p | r | y | o | a | m |
| v | a | r | c | b | j | m | q | g | h | w | a | u | a | c |
| q | y | n | d | i | j | p | x | l | o | p | l | r | d | y |
| j | p | y | o | e | s | g | f | g | r | q | t | z | e | e |
| b | c | f | d | a | r | s | l | b | k | v | e | q | v | s |
| e | o | k | f | k | s | x | o | c | p | x | r | i | o | y |
| p | v | t | h | t | o | k | f | r | m | l | a | b | u | s |
| t | e | f | c | l | n | f | q | n | e | c | t | a | r | p |
| l | r | a | x | v | z | d | k | c | t | k | n | u | z | j |

alligator     devour

rigour     nectar

scissor     alter

savour     guitar

order     metaphor

sugar     cover

**Tip**

The suffix **-ion** is used to form nouns from verbs.
For instance, the verb 'erode' becomes the noun 'erosion' and the verb 'convert' becomes the noun 'conversion'.

**If the base verb ends in *d*, *de* or *se*, replace these letters with *s* and then add the suffix -ion.**

intrude | intrusion     expand | expansion     fuse | fusion

**If the base verb ends in *ss*, just add the suffix -ion.**

compress | compression     obsess | obsession     impress | impression

**1** Read the base verbs in the first column of the table on the next page. Underline the grapheme that represents the last phoneme in each verb. Using the rules above, change each verb to a noun by adding the suffix **-ion**, and write a sentence using that word. You may use a dictionary to help you. The first one is done for you.

| Base verb | Sentence |
| --- | --- |
| colli<u>de</u> | I heard the sound of screeching car tyres immediately before the <u>collision</u>. |
| invade | |
| exclude | |
| progress | |
| comprehend | |
| include | |
| confuse | |
| confess | |

**2** Write the base verb for each of the nouns. You may use a dictionary to check the spelling of the verbs.

| Noun with *-ion* suffix | Base verb |
| --- | --- |
| conclusion | |
| erosion | |
| division | |
| explosion | |
| decision | |
| discussion | |
| revision | |
| extension | |

### Now try this unit's 'Bringing it together' activity, which your teacher will give you.

OXFORD UNIVERSITY PRESS

A compound word is a new word made out of two words joined together. The words 'sun' and 'shine' can be joined to make the compound word 'sunshine'.

## The Glimme
### by Emily Rodda

Burning with questions he could not ask, he followed the others up to the castle with his eyes on the ground. Thunder rumbled overhead, and he could hear the hum of many voices. Then he was stumbling through a doorway, and the noise was suddenly deafening.

**1** Read the text above and find words in it to complete the table.

| | |
|---|---|
| A one-syllable word ending with a **/z/** phoneme | |
| A disyllabic word starting with a consonant digraph | |
| A word rhyming with 'grumbled' | |
| All multisyllabic words with a **short /e/** phoneme | |
| Two words ... | |
| with three syllables | |
| with **/d/** as the third phoneme | |
| starting with an unvoiced **/th/** phoneme | |
| with an **/oi/** diphthong | |
| that are compound words | |
| with five phonemes | |
| with a schwa as the fourth phoneme | |

**Tip**

If the first syllable of a disyllabic word has a short vowel graph followed by one consonant letter, it is common for the medial consonant letter to be doubled. This is called a medial consonant doublet.

**1** Circle the correctly spelled disyllabic words in the table, then write the correct word in the third column. Underline the grapheme that represents the short vowel in the first syllable of each word. The first one is done for you.

| Circle the correct word | | Write the correct word | Circle the correct word | | Write the correct word |
|---|---|---|---|---|---|
| dribble | drible | dr<u>i</u>bble | narow | narrow | |
| shufle | shuffle | | torrent | torent | |
| bafle | baffle | | botle | bottle | |
| carry | cary | | ripple | riple | |
| gramar | grammar | | buter | butter | |
| hoble | hobble | | wobble | woble | |
| current | curent | | | | |

**2** Choose three words you wrote in the last activity. Write a descriptive sentence for each.

a _____

_____

b _____

_____

c _____

_____

OXFORD UNIVERSITY PRESS

**1** Read the spelling rules, which describe how the suffix **-ion** can be used to form nouns from verbs.

If the base verb ends in d, de or se, replace these letters with s and then add the suffix -ion.

suspend | suspension    collide | collision    confuse | confusion

If the base verb ends in a consonant followed by t, just add the suffix -ion.

instruct | instruction    contort | contortion    concoct | concoction

If the base verb ends in a vowel followed by t, replace the t with ss and then add the suffix -ion.

emit | emission    commit | commission    admit | admission

If the base verb ends in te, drop the e and then add the suffix -ion.
create | creation    inflate | inflation    concentrate | concentration

If the base verb ends in be, replace be with pt and then add the suffix -ion.

inscribe | inscription    prescribe | prescription    subscribe | subscription

If the base verb ends in ce, replace the e with t and then add the suffix -ion.

induce | induction    deduce | deduction    produce | production

If the base verb ends in ss, just add the suffix -ion.
depress | depression    express | expression    impress | impression

**2** Using the spelling rules about the suffix **-ion**, find the matching verbs and nouns in the words and write them in the table. Use the example to help you.

construct    reduce    pollute    permission    erode

progression    erosion    construction    progress

description    pollution    permit    reduction    describe

| Verb | Noun | Verb | Noun |
|------|------|------|------|
| comprehend | comprehension | | |
| | | | |
| | | | |
| | | | |

**3** Choose one of the nouns formed with the suffix **-ion** and one of the base verbs from the last activity. Use the noun in a sentence. Then write a new sentence using the base verb instead.

a _____

_____

b _____

_____

**Now try this unit's 'Bringing it together' activity, which your teacher will give you.**

OXFORD UNIVERSITY PRESS

# UNIT 25

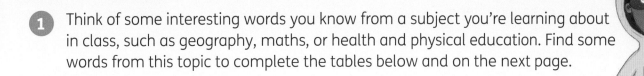

1. Think of some interesting words you know from a subject you're learning about in class, such as geography, maths, or health and physical education. Find some words from this topic to complete the tables below and on the next page.

| | |
|---|---|
| Three one-syllable words | |
| Two four-syllable words | |
| Three words with five phonemes | |
| Three words with eight phonemes | |

| | |
|---|---|
| A disyllabic word that ends with a consonant digraph | |
| A disyllabic word with an accented final syllable | |
| Two words that rhyme with a subject-specific word of your choice | Subject word:<br>Rhyming words: |

| A word ... | |
|---|---|
| with a schwa in the final syllable | |
| with an **/oi/** diphthong | |
| with a **long /o/** phoneme | |
| that ends with a vowel phoneme | |
| with a consonant digraph for the third phoneme | |

| A word ... | |
| --- | --- |
| that starts with a consonant blend | |
| with a vowel digraph | |
| with a voiced **/th/** phoneme | |
| with an unvoiced **/th/** phoneme | |

**Orthography**

1. Scan some books you are reading to find words with the **/oi/** diphthong such as 'employ' and 'rejoice'. You can also think of other words you already know with this phoneme. Complete the table below.

> **Tip**
>
> Challenge yourself by including multisyllabic words in the table.

| Words with **oy** in the initial accented syllable | |
| --- | --- |
| Words that end with **oy** | |
| Words that end with **oin** | |
| Words that end with **oice** | |
| Words that end with **oil** | |
| Words that end with **oid** | |
| Other words with the **/oi/** diphthong | |

2. Choose two of the words you wrote in the table above. Use them to write a creative sentence.

_____

_____

OXFORD UNIVERSITY PRESS

**3** Choose ten words from activity I on the previous page. Use the words to create your own word search then invite another student to complete it.

Tip

Consider adding prefixes or suffixes to some of your chosen words.

|  |  |  |  |  |  |  |  |  |  |  |  |  |  |
|--|--|--|--|--|--|--|--|--|--|--|--|--|--|
|  |  |  |  |  |  |  |  |  |  |  |  |  |  |
|  |  |  |  |  |  |  |  |  |  |  |  |  |  |
|  |  |  |  |  |  |  |  |  |  |  |  |  |  |
|  |  |  |  |  |  |  |  |  |  |  |  |  |  |
|  |  |  |  |  |  |  |  |  |  |  |  |  |  |
|  |  |  |  |  |  |  |  |  |  |  |  |  |  |
|  |  |  |  |  |  |  |  |  |  |  |  |  |  |
|  |  |  |  |  |  |  |  |  |  |  |  |  |  |
|  |  |  |  |  |  |  |  |  |  |  |  |  |  |
|  |  |  |  |  |  |  |  |  |  |  |  |  |  |

Words to find in the word search:

_____  _____  _____

_____  _____  _____

_____  _____

Tip

The suffix **-ation** can be used to form nouns from verbs. For example, the noun 'reservation' can be formed from the verb 'reserve'.

**If the base verb ends in *y*, it is common to replace the *y* with *ic* and then add the suffix -*ation*.**

imply | implication     multiply | multiplication     apply | application

**If the base verb ends in *re*, *ve* or *se*, it is common to remove the *e* and then add the suffix -*ation*.**

reserve | reservation     expire | expiration     improvise | improvisation

**1** Using the spelling rules about the suffix **-ation**, find the matching verbs and nouns in the words and write them in the table. One has been done for you.

| magnification | organise | inspire | organisation | classification | magnify |

| identify | identification | ~~preparation~~ | conserve | inspiration |

| conservation | simplification | ~~prepare~~ | simplify | classify |

| Verb | Noun |
|------|------|
| prepare | preparation |
|  |  |
|  |  |
|  |  |
|  |  |
|  |  |
|  |  |

**2** Choose one of the nouns formed with the suffix **-ation** and one of the base verbs from the last activity. Use both of these words in a sentence.

_____

_____

Now try this unit's 'Bringing it together' activity, which your teacher will give you.

OXFORD UNIVERSITY PRESS

# UNIT 26

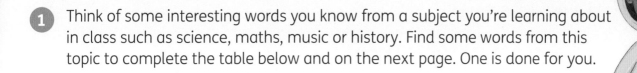

**1** Think of some interesting words you know from a subject you're learning about in class such as science, maths, music or history. Find some words from this topic to complete the table below and on the next page. One is done for you.

| | |
|---|---|
| Three words with seven phonemes | |
| Three words with eight phonemes | |
| Three words with nine phonemes | |
| A disyllabic word with an unaccented final syllable | |
| A disyllabic word with an accented final syllable | |
| A disyllabic word that ends with a consonant digraph | |
| A multisyllabic word with a schwa in the first syllable | |
| Two words that rhyme with a subject-specific word of your choice | Subject word:<br>Rhyming words: |
| **A word ...** | |
| with more than four syllables | |
| that has the same phoneme twice | |
| with an **/oi/** diphthong | |
| with a **long /o/** phoneme | |

| A word ... | |
| --- | --- |
| that ends with a vowel phoneme | |
| with a consonant digraph for the third phoneme | |
| that starts with a consonant blend | |
| that ends with a consonant blend | |
| with a vowel digraph | |
| with a **/z/** phoneme | |
| with a **/s/** phoneme | |

1 Choose ten words from the last activity. Use the words to create your own word search then invite another student to complete it.

**Tip**

Consider adding prefixes or suffixes to some of your chosen words.

Words to find in the word search:

_____   _____   _____

_____   _____   _____

_____

OXFORD UNIVERSITY PRESS

**2** Scan some books you are reading to find words such as 'ground' with the phoneme **/ow/**, as in 'how'. You can also think of other words you already know with this phoneme. Complete the table.

| | | | |
|---|---|---|---|
| Words ending in **ow** | | | |
| Words ending in **own** | | | |
| Words ending in **ower** | | | |
| Words ending in **ount** | | | |
| Words ending in **ounce** | | | |
| Words ending in **ouse** | | | |
| Words ending in **oud** | | | |
| Words ending in **ound** | | | |

Tip

The suffix **-ise** means 'to cause' or 'to become'. This is the way the suffix is spelled in Australian and British English. The Standard American spelling for this suffix is **-ize**. You might notice that some words are spelled differently if you are reading something from the United States or Canada.

**Morphology**

**1** Read the words in the first column of each table below and on the next page and write the base word they are formed from. The first one has been done for you.

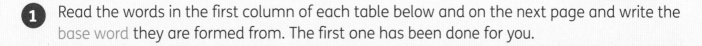

**If the base word ends in e or y, drop the e or y and add the suffix -ise.**
satire | satirise      accessory | accessorise      category | categorise

| Word with suffix | Base word | Word with suffix | Base word |
|---|---|---|---|
| standardise | standard | materialise | |
| characterise | | vocalise | |

| Word with suffix | Base word | Word with suffix | Base word |
|---|---|---|---|
| criticise | | memorise | |
| specialise | | fertilise | |

2. Choose one word with a suffix from the table above and write a sentence using that word.

_____

_____

Tip

An affix is a prefix or suffix that can be added to a base word. An affix always counts as a morpheme because it is a part of a word that carries meaning. Some base words can form new words with more than one affix. The word 'unbelievably' has three affixes: the prefix **un-** and the suffixes **-able** and **-ly**.

3. Build as many new words as you can by adding affixes to the base word 'character'. Some of the new words will have one affix and others will have several affixes.

| Prefix | Base word | Suffixes | | | | New words |
|---|---|---|---|---|---|---|
| **un-** | character | **-s** | **-ise** | **-ing** | **-able** | |
| | | | **-istic** | **-ed** | **-ation** | |
| | | | | | **-ally** | |

Now try this unit's 'Bringing it together' activity, which your teacher will give you.

OXFORD UNIVERSITY PRESS

# UNIT 27

1. Scan a book you are reading to find interesting or unusual words to complete this table. One is done for you.

| Three disyllabic words | |
| A disyllabic word that ends with a consonant digraph | |
| Two three-syllable words | |
| Two four-syllable words | |
| A five-syllable word | |
| A multisyllabic word with two schwas | |
| Three words with eight phonemes | |
| Three words with nine phonemes | |
| A disyllabic word that ends with a consonant digraph | |
| A disyllabic word with an unaccented final syllable | |
| A disyllabic word with an accented final syllable | |
| A word with a schwa in the third syllable | |

| Two words that rhyme | |
|---|---|
| A word ... | |
| with more than ten phonemes | |
| with the **long /oo/** phoneme | |
| with the **short /oo/** phoneme | |
| that ends with a vowel phoneme | |
| with a consonant digraph to represent the third phoneme | |
| that starts with a consonant blend | |
| that ends with a consonant blend | |
| with a vowel digraph | |

**1** Scan a book you are reading to find words with the **/f/** phoneme, as in 'feet'. You can also think of other words you already know with this phoneme. Complete the table.

| **f** | feather |
|---|---|
| **ff** | gruff |
| **ph** | photosynthesis |
| **gh** | rough |

**2** Choose ten words from the last activity. Use the words to create your own word search then invite a classmate to complete it.

Consider adding prefixes or suffixes to some of your chosen words.

| | | | | | | | | | | | | |
|---|---|---|---|---|---|---|---|---|---|---|---|---|
| | | | | | | | | | | | | |
| | | | | | | | | | | | | |
| | | | | | | | | | | | | |
| | | | | | | | | | | | | |
| | | | | | | | | | | | | |
| | | | | | | | | | | | | |
| | | | | | | | | | | | | |
| | | | | | | | | | | | | |
| | | | | | | | | | | | | |
| | | | | | | | | | | | | |

Words to find in the word search:

_____   _____   _____

_____   _____   _____

_____   _____

_____   _____

Some prefixes are partially absorbed (or assimilated) into a base word. This happens when the last letter of the prefix is replaced by the first letter of the base word. The table lists some prefixes, and explains how they are assimilated.

| Prefix | Meaning | First letter of base word | Example |
|---|---|---|---|
| **in-** | 'not', 'the opposite', or 'without' | **l**, **n**, **m** or **r** | **in** + legal = illegal |
| **com-** | 'with' or 'together' | **c**, **l**, **n** or **r** | **com** + league = colleague |
| **ad-** | 'to' or 'toward' | **c**, **f** or **p** | **ad** + prove = approve |

**1** Complete the table on the next page. You may use a dictionary if you are not sure what a word means.

| Prefix | Base word | Word with affix | Prefix | Base word | Word with affix |
|--------|-----------|-----------------|--------|-----------|-----------------|
| *in-* | legal | illegal | *com-* | note | |
| *com-* | league | colleague | *in-* | rational | |
| *ad-* | prove | approve | *in-* | mature | |
| *com-* | respond | | *ad-* | count | |
| *in-* | logical | | *com-* | relate | |
| *ad-* | claim | | *com-* | lapse | |
| *ad-* | praise | | *in-* | responsible | |
| *in-* | mobile | | *ad-* | firm | |

**2** Choose four words that you wrote in the table above. Write a sentence for each one.

a  _____

_____

b  _____

_____

c  _____

_____

d  _____

_____

**Now try this unit's 'Bringing it together' activity, which your teacher will give you.**

OXFORD UNIVERSITY PRESS

# UNIT 28

**1** Scan a book you are reading to find interesting or unusual words to complete this table. One is done for you.

| | |
|---|---|
| A word with five syllables | |
| A multisyllabic word with two schwas | |
| A word with ten phonemes | |
| A disyllabic word that ends with a consonant digraph | |
| A disyllabic word with an accented final syllable | |
| A multisyllabic word with a schwa in the third syllable | |
| A multisyllabic word with a **long /e/** phoneme | |
| Two words that rhyme | |
| A word ... | |
| with three different vowel phonemes | |
| that ends with a vowel phoneme | |
| with a consonant digraph to represent the third phoneme | |
| that ends with a consonant blend | |

1 Choose ten words from the last activity. Use the words to create your own word search then invite a classmate to complete it.

**Tip**

Why not try adding prefixes or suffixes to some of your chosen words?

Words to find in the word search:

_____    _____    _____

_____    _____    _____

_____    _____

_____    _____

2 Scan a book you are reading to find words with the **/g/** phoneme, such as 'go' and 'ghee'. You can also think of other words you know with this phoneme. Complete the table.

| | |
|---|---|
| **g** | girl |
| **gg** | smuggle |
| **gh** | gherkin |
| **gue** | plague |

OXFORD UNIVERSITY PRESS

**1** Use the word matrix below to build as many new words as you can by adding affixes to the base word 'form'. Some of the new words will have one affix and others will have several affixes.

| Prefixes | Base word | Suffixes | New words |
|----------|-----------|----------|-----------|
| *in-*    | form      | *-s*     |           |
| *re-*    |           | *-ed*    |           |
| *de-*    |           | *-ing*   |           |
|          |           | *-er*    |           |
|          |           | *-ation* |           |
|          |           | *-al*    |           |

**2** Now create your own word matrix. First, select a base word. List possible prefixes and suffixes that could be added to that base word. Then list as many words with affixes as you can think of.

| Prefixes | Base word | Suffixes | New words |
|----------|-----------|----------|-----------|
|          |           |          |           |

**Now try this unit's 'Bringing it together' activity, which your teacher will give you.**

# GLOSSARY

| | |
|---|---|
| **accented syllable** | the syllable in a word that has the strongest emphasis<br>*the first syllable in 'apple' and the second syllable in 'believe'* |
| **adjective** | a word that tells us what something is like<br>*small, tall, funny* |
| **base word** | the smallest part of a word that is also a word on its own<br>*the word 'jump' in 'jumping'* |
| **blend** | speech sounds that join together in a word<br>*/st/ is a blend in the word 'stop'* |
| **consonant** | a speech sound made by blocking some air with your lips, teeth or tongue<br>**/b/, /l/, /z/, /v/** |
| **consonant digraph** | two letters representing one consonant sound<br>**sh**, **ch**, **th** |
| **digraph** | two letters representing one phoneme<br>**sh**, **ch**, **oo**, **ee**, **ie** |
| **diphthong** | a kind of long vowel sound that you make by moving your mouth in two ways<br>**/oi/** *in 'boy',* **/ow/** *in 'cow'* |
| **disyllabic word** | a word with two syllables<br>*monster (mon-ster), sunshine (sun-shine)* |
| **etymology** | the study of where words come from and how they change over time<br>*the word 'pizza' comes from a Latin word and an Italian dialect word meaning to clamp or stamp* |
| **graph** | one letter representing one phoneme<br>**b**, **w**, **o** |
| **grapheme** | a letter or group of letters representing one phoneme<br>**a**, **sh**, **tch** |
| **homophone** | a word that sounds the same as another word but looks different and has a different meaning<br>*eight, ate* |
| **medial** | in the middle. A medial phoneme is a speech sound in the middle of a word. This can be a medial vowel or a medial consonant.<br>**/o/** *is the medial phoneme in 'dog'* |
| **medial consonant doublet** | a doubled consonant letter in the middle of a word<br>**bb** *in 'bubble'* |
| **morpheme** | the smallest unit of meaning in a word<br>*'jumped' has two parts with meaning (**jump** and **-ed**)* |
| **multisyllabic word** | a word with more than one syllable<br>*chamber (cham-ber), trampoline (tram-po-line)* |

OXFORD UNIVERSITY PRESS

| | |
|---|---|
| **noun** | a word that is a name for something, such as a person, place, animal, thing or idea<br>*Ali, school, cat, ball, age, protection* |
| **phoneme** | the smallest speech sound you can hear in a word<br>*the word 'boot' has three phonemes: **/b/**, **long /oo/** and **/t/**.* |
| **plural** | a word for more than one thing<br>*'hats' is the plural of the word 'hat'* |
| **prefix** | letters that go at the beginning of a word to make a new word<br>***un** in 'unhappy' means 'not' (**un** + happy = not happy)* |
| **quadgraph** | four letters representing one phoneme<br>***eigh** in 'eight'* |
| **rime** | the vowel and other speech sounds at the end of a syllable<br>***ig** represents the rime in the word 'big'* |
| **r-influenced vowel phoneme** | a vowel that sounds different because it is followed by the letter ***r***<br>***/er/** in 'mermaid', **/air/** in 'pear'* |
| **schwa** | an **/uh/** sound in a word<br>*the **a** in 'balloon' and the **our** in 'colour' represent an **/uh/** sound* |
| **suffix** | letters that go at the end of a word to make a new word<br>*the **-ful** in 'powerful' means 'full of', so 'powerful' means 'full of power'* |
| **syllable** | a part of a word that feels like a beat and has a vowel sound<br>*'weekend' has two syllables (week-end)* |
| **syllable juncture** | the place in a word where two syllables meet<br>*in the word 'return', the syllable juncture is between the **e** and the **t*** |
| **tense** | the way a word is written that shows whether something is in the past, present or future<br>*'I walked' is in past tense, 'I walk' is in present tense, 'I will walk' is in future tense* |
| **trigraph** | three letters representing one phoneme<br>***igh** in 'might'* |
| **unvoiced phoneme** | a sound made using your breath rather than your voice<br>***/th/** in 'thunder', **/p/** in 'past', **/s/** in 'chess'* |
| **verb** | a word for something that happens<br>*'play' is the verb in the sentence 'I play chess.'* |
| **voiced phoneme** | a sound made using your voice<br>***/th/** in 'that', **/b/** and **/g/** in bag* |
| **vowel** | a sound that you voice with your mouth open and not blocked by your lips, teeth or tongue<br>*the **short /o/** sound in the word 'dog' is a vowel sound* |

When you have finished the activities in each unit, think about how you feel about the work you have completed.

Draw a ✓ if you feel confident using these ideas on your own.

Draw a ✗ if you feel you need to learn more.

Draw a ○ if you are not sure.

| Unit | Phonology | Orthography | Morphology |
|------|-----------|-------------|------------|
| 1 | | | |
| 2 | | | |
| 3 | | | |
| 4 | | | |
| 5 | | | |
| 6 | | | |
| 7 | | | |
| 8 | | | |
| 9 | | | |
| 10 | | | |
| 11 | | | |
| 12 | | | |
| 13 | | | |
| 14 | | | |
| 15 | | | |
| 16 | | | |
| 17 | | | |
| 18 | | | |
| 19 | | | |
| 20 | | | |
| 21 | | | |
| 22 | | | |
| 23 | | | |
| 24 | | | |
| 25 | | | |
| 26 | | | |
| 27 | | | |
| 28 | | | |

OXFORD UNIVERSITY PRESS